A Woman of Vision

by Kitane Elder

DORRANCE PUBLISHING CO
EST. 1920
PITTSBURGH, PENNSYLVANIA 15238

Dorrance Publishing Co
585 Alpha Drive
Suite 103
Pittsburgh, PA 15238
Visit our website at *www.dorrancebookstore.com*

ISBN: 979-8-8860-4120-0
eISBN: 979-8-8860-4785-1

A Woman of Vision

DEDICATION

A special thank you to our late dog Shadow. He was always there to cuddle while I wrote this story. This is to you and your spitefulness. We miss you!

CHAPTER ONE

It was her sixth birthday party. Balloons were tied to the mailbox, Barbie dolls scattered in the yard, silly string up and down the driveway, and little kids' laughter and squeals coming from the backyard.

Well, the day had gone off without a hitch, everyone looked to be happy and enjoying themselves. It was especially nice to see Cristina and Katelyn having fun with their friends and loving the party. All the dads were drinking beers and cracking jokes while moms were sipping wine under the canopy. It had been a couple of hours but David had been inside for a while. *I might as well get everyone inside so I can clean up a little bit and we can open the gifts.*

As if we were in sync David popped his head out of the sliding glass door to shout, "It's present time! Everyone inside and gather around the couch, please."

Everyone started to filter inside as I cleaned up the backyard. Grabbing beer cans and wine glasses on my way in.

David walked over with a frown on his face. "What crazy aunt did you invite to the party?!" he asked roughly.

"What do you mean, baby?" I asked.

"Janet, stop playing games with me. Some women stopped by to tell us Cris is in danger. What kind of sick game are you playing?!"

"Wait, what's going on? Who is this woman, is she still here?! What did she say to you?"

"She said later in life she will need protection, that we need to prepare to go into hiding and leave before she turns 16. At first I thought she was talking about teenage pregnancy. You really had nothing to do with this?" he said with a confused look.

"Of course not, David! I'm not sure what she was talking about...come on, let's go inside. We can talk about this later. The girls are getting antsy."

We walked inside to watch Cristina open gifts.

Chapter Two

Dec. 29th, 2020

Looking into the mirror in my bedroom, trying to fix my hair, I grumbled, "I'm going to be late. Hmm, why can't I get my hair to chill out?"

"Cris, am I driving you to school or are you catching the bus?"

"I'll catch the bus, Dad, I'm not ready yet but thanks. Love ya!" I shouted back.

Listening to him walk out the front door without kissing Mom goodbye again. He got in his truck and drove to work.

"Alright, finishing touches and done," I said as I walked toward the kitchen. I stopped briefly when I saw Mom standing in the doorway of Katelyn's room. "Mom, you can't keep doing this. Katelyn is gone. She's not coming back. Come on, let's get some food into you. Okay?"

I reached out for her arm and led her into the kitchen. Found her a seat at the dining room table and she put her head into her hands, quietly sobbing. Trying not to cry, I grabbed some eggs from the fridge.

Placing the eggs in a pot of water, I gently asked, "Hey, Mom? Would you like to talk about it?" waiting for the same conversation we had every morning since I was six years old.

Mom looked up from her hands with tear streaks down her face. "I just don't know what happened. One minute I'm standing in the doorway in her room while she's looking for her favorite book for bedtime and the next she's just gone. I went outside to look for the book just in case it had been left outside from the party and when I came back...." Her words trailed off as if she was reliving the moment. "I wasn't gone for more than five minutes, I'm sure. But my baby. She's gone. She's gone and it's my fault," she whispered in between sobs.

"Mom, stop. It's not your fault." Trying to console her, I got up and leaned down for a hug.

Rocking back and forth, she started talking to herself. "David warned me but the lady mentioned Cris, not Katelyn. She said it would be later in life, not then. I should've listened, I should've protected her. I shouldn't have left her," she said quietly to herself.

I stood up slowly and let go of my mother. I had never heard this part of the conversation. It was such a faint whisper it almost missed my ears. This was unbelievable.

"Who are you talking about? What do you mean Dad warned you?" I demanded.

She started to calm down and explain. "You probably don't remember your sixth birthday party. That day was perfect, you and your sister were having so much fun playing in the backyard with the neighbor kids. After the party we were doing our bedtime routine. We had gotten everything done except the bedtime story. You were already tucked in bed and asleep. You never did like bedtime stories but Katelyn loved them. Every night she would pick out a book. That night she wanted to read *Peanut Butter and Cupcake*, her favorite book. We went into her room to read it but it wasn't on her bookshelf. I told her to get in bed and I would go and look for it. I remembered she had brought it outside to show Uncle Mike that afternoon during the party. Maybe it had been left outside. I walked back into her bedroom to tell her I couldn't find it and she was gone. I figured she probably went to the bathroom before getting in bed and she would be back in a second. A few minutes passed and she still hadn't come back. Maybe she didn't go to the bathroom and went to say goodnight to your father. Again I was wrong. She wasn't anywhere in the house. She was gone. We checked with the neighbors and called the police. We went outside and called her name. But she was just gone. According to your father, there was a woman that showed up on our doorstep during the party. She spoke with your father and warned him of her vision from the night before. We didn't believe her, we didn't heed her warning and that night your sister went missing." Frustrated, she spat.

"Did you tell the cops about the woman? Do you know who she is? Why didn't I know about this?!"

She responded with "Sadly, baby girl, I never saw her. Your father did, though. He gave a description to the police. He said she had brown, straight hair to about here," she said, pointing to the crook of her elbow. "Blue eyes and she was 5'7", I believe he said. The police have no leads. They said the first 48 hours are the most crucial and by 72 hours it becomes more difficult. But it's been eight years and my baby still isn't home. The case is still open...," she trailed off. "I'm not in the mood for eggs today, sweetie. I think I'll just go lie down and try to get some rest. Do you want me to call an Uber for you so you can get to school? I think you missed the bus," she said, sounding exhausted.

"Um, no, I'm fine, Mom. Thanks. I think I'll call Carter and see if he's busy. Is it okay if I skip school today? I'm, uh, not feeling so good," I said, depressed.

"Of course, honey, your birthday is tomorrow and it's a Friday. I think it'll be fine."

Carter Stevens was my best guy friend. He was homeschooled. Knew four languages (English, Spanish, German, French) and was very intelligent and mature for his age, which was 17. He drove a gray Jeep Wrangler and had a sister named Jennifer. His mother was a Marine (Staff Sergeant) Lisa Fowler. Father was "an accountant," Joseph Stevens.

I grabbed my bag from beside the front door and slipped out, locking it behind me. I started walking the direction of Carter's house as my phone rang in my back pocket. Pulling it out, the caller ID read "Meredith." I answered with "Hello?"

"Where are you?! We've decked out your locker and we're all waiting. The bell is about to go off, you better not be ditching."

With a flat tone I said, "Hey, Meredith. I'm not ditching. *cough cough* I'm sick," I pretended while imitating a hoarse scratchy voice. "I'm not coming in today. Thank you for the surprise but I'm home in bed." Pretending Mom was in my room checking my temperature. "What? 101 temp? Oh, my gosh. Thanks for the soup, Mom, it smells great. Okay, gotta go, Mer, bye," and I hung up.

Scrolling through my recently called list to find Carter's number, I pushed the call button and waited for the calling tone.

"What's up, birthday girl?"

I smiled and said, "Hey, can you pick me up? I'm on my way to—"

My words cut off when I realized a Jeep was pulling up behind me. The Jeep pulled over to the side of the road and I looked to see who was driving. It was Carter.

"Hey, need a ride?"

Still smiling, I jumped in and said, "Thanks."

With a big grin he said, "Fancy seeing you here. Aren't you supposed to be at school?"

"Yes, but I kinda need your help...,"

"Always," he said and drove off.

CHAPTER THREE

Back Story

> <u>Narrator:</u> Katelyn was taken by a woman named Naomi, who trained her as security detail. Naomi had been taught by her mother (the Great Escapetress), both of whom had the premonition gift. She told Katelyn that her sister Cris was destined for greatness and her role was to protect her sister from all those short-sighted. She needed to come with her to train and learn the ways of safety, security, and sacrifice. Katelyn went willingly.

Now that her sister turned 16 tomorrow it was time for her to return home and assume her position as security detail. Something special about Cris that no one knew but Katelyn and Naomi. Her sister would be the next president. Over the years the laws of office changed, you no longer had to be 35 years or older to run. The laws put in place allowed 18+ to run for office. Her sister would be the next president. Her sister would help the world become a better place for everyone and everything. Setting off, she said goodbye to her friends and Naomi. She hopped on a bus and was back in her hometown in a matter of hours. Her mom had been so distraught over the years hoping and praying to hear any news of her little girl's disappearance. The mother no longer worked due to this crimpling loss. She would stay home and stand in the doorway of her little girl's room. The last place she saw her. Standing there she realized her hands were tingling. Thinking it was poor circulation from not eating enough and standing for hours on end, she headed toward the kitchen and she felt herself being pulled to the side door. She was confused and stood there for a moment. She jumped as she heard a knock on the door. She walked to the side door wiping her tears away. Opening the door she saw a young lady standing there with a duffel bag.

"How can I help you?" she said while sniffling.

The young lady said, "Hi, Mom."

With a puzzled look on her face, Janet straightened. "Excuse me?"

"Mom, it's me, Katelyn."

CHAPTER FOUR

Narrator: Cris and Carter went to a coffee shop around the corner from his house. Sitting there sipping coffee, they talked.

Cris: "What do you know about the night my sister disappeared?"

Carter: "Uh, okay. That's out of the blue. I remember my mom getting a call from your mom asking if she was at our house. My mom ran in my room and asked if I had seen Katelyn since we left your party. It was a little frightening because we were all there, the kidnapper could've taken any one of us. Now that I think about it, it's weird they took your sister but not you...."

Cris: "Yeah, don't get me started on the guilt I feel for that. Maybe if I had been awake she would've taken me...."

Carter: "Cris, stop. You can't blame yourself."

Cris: "All I know is my mom spilled the beans about the kidnapper this morning and it's all I can think about."

Carter: "What do you mean?"

Cris: "My mom said a lady came to the house and told my dad that I was in danger and then Katelyn goes missing. What if they thought she was me?! What if Katelyn's dead because of me?!" Cris said frantically.

Carter: "Hold on, you can't think that way. I'm sure Katelyn is just fine. Just breathe, Cris, and drink your hot cocoa. Did your mom tell you why you were in danger?"

Cris: "It's all confusing, she wasn't making a lot of sense by this point in the conversation. Anyways, I'm not important here, Katelyn is the one missing. I just—" Cris stopped talking when her phone rang again. The caller ID read "Mom." She pushed the red decline button and put her phone away. "I just need to know what happened to my sister."

Chapter Five

Narrator: 4:45 P.M. rolled around. David was home from work, he pulled into the driveway and sat in his truck for a few minutes. He looked very sad and slowly he started to gather his belongings and get out. He unlocked the front door and went inside. He called out for Cris and got no response. Looking around he muttered about how dark it was in the house and why there were never any lights on when he came home. He headed to the kitchen to get dinner started, flipping switches as he went. When he turned the corner and saw his wife and a young lady holding hands sitting at the kitchen table.

David: "Janet, who's this?"

Janet: Janet turned around with tears streaming down her face. She jumped up and threw herself at David and shouted, "It's our daughter! She's come back to us! David, I thought we would never see her again!"

David: David hugged Janet for the first time in years and looked past her to the young woman standing up. "I'm sorry, what? No, this. This isn't happening, I must be dreaming...Katelyn? Baby girl, is that really you?" he stuttered with eyes watering up. He tried to hold back the tears but a flood of emotions hit him for just the possibility of seeing his little girl again.

Narrator: Janet pulled herself together and let go of David. David wiped his eyes and walked toward Katelyn with his arms open, ready for a hug to cement the idea into his head. His daughter was home and the hole in his heart was gone. Katelyn hugged her father and started to cry, not realizing how much she had actually missed her family.

Outside Carter pulled his jeep into the driveway and let Cris out. He handed her bag over and said he would see her later and to tell her family he said hello. She agreed, said goodbye, and walked toward the house. Once inside she dropped her bag by the front door and walked to the kitchen.

Cris: "Hey, Dad, do you need help with dinner?" She walked around the corner and into the kitchen to find her dad hugging a woman. "Hey...what's going on?"

Narrator: Both of her parents were crying, her dad let go of Katelyn and reached for the towel hanging on the stove handle and wiped away the tears from his face. Katelyn smiled and said, "Hey, big sister."

CHAPTER SIX

Narrator: Cris and Katelyn were sitting in the living room catching up while their parents were outside explaining Katelyn's return to the police.

Cris: Cris walked into the living room from the kitchen carrying two bottles of water. She handed one to Katelyn and sat on the couch. "Look. I need to know what happened to you. I've been feeling guilty ever since that night. So spill the beans."

Katelyn: Took a sip and put the cap back on. With concern plastered on her face, she looked Cris in the eyes and said, "I know you want to know the details but... maybe we should wait until Mom and Dad come back inside before we talk about it. It's about all of us." Trying to change the subject she blurted, "So tell me about your life, I'm so excited to hear what all is going on!"

Cris: "Ah, just the normal stuff. Friends, school, Mom being a total vegetable due to your disappearance.... Damn, I'm sorry. That was a low blow. It's just been really hard here without you. I've been doing well in school because it's an escape from this house. Mom stands in your doorway all day and all night just staring at the bookcase. She said that's the last place she saw you. She barely eats. Me and Dad pretty much take care of everything. We cook, clean, he pays the bills. We almost lost the house after Mom stopped working. Dad had to get two jobs just to bridge the gap until he found this job. Now he just works the one and we can afford everything again but the last nine years have been really tough. We didn't know for sure if you were even still alive. Your room is the same, by the way. We didn't move anything. I guess, though, since you aren't six anymore we'll need to update a few things. We can probably go shopping tomorrow. Is your favorite color still green?"

Narrator: Janet and David were followed through the front door by a police officer. They all walked into the living room.

Janet: "Katelyn, sweetheart. This nice policeman is here to get a statement from you about what happened," she said with a smile.

Police Officer: "Hello, I'm Officer Oliver Stanton. What's your name?"

Katelyn: "Hello, my name is Katelyn Maria Moore. It's nice to meet you, Officer Stanton."

Police Officer/Oliver Stanton: Jotting down notes as they talked. "It's my pleasure. We thought we had lost you. Can you remember what happened the night you disappeared?"

Katelyn: "There was a man hiding under my bed...he crawled out and grabbed me. I remember there was a black truck. He threw me in and he drove away. He hit me in the face and I guess I blacked out because I don't remember the drive to the house. I just remember waking up in the basement. He starved me and tied me to a chair. It was dark and cold. I finally escaped a year ago when someone broke in and robbed the place.

Whoever it was shot the man. I heard yelling and demands being made, then a gunshot and things breaking. It sounded like they were going through the house and tossing it. But then it got really quiet and I heard someone running out of the house. I guess maybe they got spooked or something. I was so terrified but I kept trying to break my restraints. When I finally did, I made my way upstairs, they were gone and my captor was dead by the front door. So I ran. I didn't have any money or food and I didn't want to get blamed for his murder. All I had were the clothes I was wearing and they were torn and too small. I wandered around for a day or so until a woman offered me a place to sleep, food, and warm clothes. She was really nice. Later she offered me a job at her bakery. I was able to make enough to save for a ticket home. Turns out I was in Oregon. That's really all I remember, Officer. Is that enough for the statement? I'm very tired and would like to spend time with my family."

Police Officer/Oliver Stanton: "Yes, that is enough. Thank you. I am truly sorry you had to go through that and that we weren't able to help more. I'm glad you're home, Katelyn. Goodnight, all, I'll let myself out."

Narrator: Saying goodnight, the police officer left. Janet, David, and Cris had horrified looks on their faces. They all looked around at each other as to say this was going to take a lot of therapy. Katelyn stood up and walked to stand in front of them all.

Katelyn: "Okay, I know that was a lot for you guys to hear. I need you to know. None of it was true. It was a cover story to get the cops off our case because we have a more pressing matter that we need to handle without police interference. Mom and Dad, Cris is special. She is going to be the next President of the United States. Once the world finds out there will be hundreds of assassins after her. My job is to protect her. That is why

I disappeared. The lady that came and warned you on Cris' birthday. This is what she was talking about. That lady was the mother of the woman whom I left with that night. Understand I went willingly. She explained that Cris would need me to protect her while she protected the United States of America." Looking at Cris she said, "You are so special, big sister, and you are going to change the world."

Narrator: The room exploded with questions from David and Janet. The whys, the how-could-yous, the are-you-serious? But not a word came from Cris. She just sat there silent and thinking.

David: "Okay, Katelyn, enough joking around. It's not funny. No daughter of ours would be stupid enough to go with a stranger willingly like that. I'm sorry if you were traumatized by that man but there is no excuse for making up such an absurd story."

Cris: "Dad. I believe her. Over the last year I've realized that the U.S. is declining in its leadership. That the wrong choices are being made and it is harming society and our civilization. Something has to be done...." She trailed off as she remembered something. "I had a dream last night that I was president and the people were happy again. That the world was a better place. I didn't remember it until now.... You know what? I'm in!" she shouted with exuberance.

<h1 style="text-align:center">CHAPTER SEVEN</h1>

<u>Narrator:</u> After a lot of discussion the whole family got on board, they all packed their bags to leave. They loaded up in the dad's truck.

<u>David:</u> "So where are we going to go? No one even knows she will be president yet so why do we need to run?!"

<u>Katelyn:</u> "Because there are other seers in the fold. The moment she turns 16 is the moment they will know she is the next president. We need to hide her now. I'll direct you on where we're going. I secured a nice little place for us to stay low and out of sight for a few years."

<u>Mom:</u> "Years?! What are you talking about, why years?!"

<u>Katelyn:</u> "Look, I am the one fated to protect my sister. If you aren't on board then get out of the truck. I have a plan and it will work. I've seen it."

<u>David:</u> "Kate, we're on board, this is just a lot thrown at us in a short timeframe and it's something we need time to adapt to. You've been training for this for what...nine years now. We've known about this for 45 minutes."

<u>Cris:</u> "I think we all just need some quiet time to think about things. Maybe we should listen to Christmas music."

<u>Katelyn:</u> "Cristina, it's August."

<u>Cris:</u> Cringing, she said, "Oh, um. It's something that we did after you were taken or, uh, left. I don't know how it made you guys feel but it made me feel better like I hadn't just lost my sister, but instead it made me think about the last Christmas we had together. We were all so happy."

<u>Katelyn:</u> "Oh, wow. I'm sorry, you guys, I never thought about how you would feel when I left or how you would feel when I came back. Jesus, I'm so selfish. I can't believe I did that."

CHAPTER EIGHT

Narrator: Everyone got out of the car when Katelyn whispered, "We're here."

Janet: "I don't think we're in the right place...maybe we should just get a hotel room or something."

Katelyn: "No, we're here."

Janet: "Okay, Kate, where is here? All I see is dirt," she said, looking around.

Katelyn: "You guys probably can't see it but it's there," she said and pointed. "Hurry, it's ten minutes till your birthday. If we get you in here they won't be able to see you let alone track you."

Narrator: Everyone grabbed their bags and rushed over where Katelyn was standing.

Cris: "Where?"

Narrator: She grabbed everyone's hand individually and walked them through the barrier, at which they disappeared. First to go was Cris due to importance. Then everyone else at once since it seemed to freak out the parentals.

Janet: "What was that? Why did she disappear?!"

Katelyn: "Short answer...magic. I didn't want to tell you guys because you were already overwhelmed by the whole president thing but now's as good a time as ever. Magic exists. The creatures in the fairytales are real. At least now we all have a safe place to talk these things out," she said as she gestured to the small shed they were all standing in.

David: "Wait, you expect the four of us to live here for years? You are kidding, right?"

Katelyn: "No. I mean, yes. Well, not in the shed. This is just the entrance," she said with a giggle.

Narrator: Katelyn walked to the back of the shed, moved a rug off the floor, and there was a secret door that led to a stairwell. They all walked down the first flight of stairs to see a huge underground bunker, fully equipped with everything they would need for the next five years. Not that they would need five years' worth of stuff but there it was, their saving grace. No need for grocery trips, there was a fully stocked kitchen, nursery, and livestock in the underground pastures. There were several entertainment rooms for a variety of fun things to see and do.

Katelyn: I'm so grateful we made it here on time. Happy birthday, sis!

Chapter Nine

Narrator: Things seemed to settle down as everyone unpacked and went to have alone time. Katelyn walked the grounds to make sure everything was secure and safe. She ended her watch in the kitchen, where Giovanni was preparing dinner for the family.

Katelyn: "Hey, how's it coming?"

Giovanni: "It's great! I'm glad you all made it here safely."

Katelyn: "Me too. Hey, do you wanna spar later tonight, after dinner maybe? I've got a lot of built-up tension from today."

Giovanni: "KatieKat, I'm always down to kick your butt," he said, laughing.

Katelyn started to blush.

Katelyn: "Ha, well, you can try. I better go check on everyone. See ya later, Geo," she said with a smile.

Katelyn: Walking away she mumbled to herself, "Why can't I just tell him I like him? It's not hard, you just have to do it. Nerves. That's why. I can kick bad guy butt but

I can't tell Geo I like him. Greeeaat." Trying to hide her mortified look, she walked into the common room and picked up a throw pillow and slumped down on the couch. "Why can't I just make things easy on myself?"

Cris: "Uh-oh...I think she might be terminal. Look at her, she's practically dying," she said with a giggle. "What's wrong?" Cris said as her and Janet walked into the room.

Katelyn: "I like him and yet here I am like a potato on the couch when I should be making out on it. What do I do?! I can't tell him I like him because then he will hear me but I want him to know."

Janet: "Wait, who?"

Katelyn: "Geo."

Cris: "Oh, is that who that is? I couldn't figure out why we were hiding but had a personal chef. Well, at least he's cute."

Katelyn: "Ahhh. He is more than cute," she said as she sprung up clutching the pillow. "He's sweet. He's smart, amazingly handsome. Plus we've spent pretty much every day together since I was six."

Cris: "Wait. He was with you? All that time he was there and you still never made a move?! Girl, if you don't get off this couch and go talk to him I will," she said jokingly.

Janet: "I'm not sure if you want an old woman's opinion but here it is. If you two have spent that much time together and he doesn't like you like that, then that's okay, sweety. No one will know unless you ask him out. Boys, well. Most of the male population aren't very... how do you say open to signals when it comes to relationships. You pretty much have to hit them over the head with it. Like your father, for instance. We were together for three years until I finally asked him if we were ever going to get married. He blushed and got down on one knee. He had the ring in his pocket every day for two years but never asked because he didn't know if I would say yes."

Katelyn: "Yeah, you're right, that's super simple," she said sarcastically. "Unless he says no he isn't interested at all, which I make a fool of myself and the tension gets too heavy and he leaves. Nope, I can't do it."

Cris: "You can do it. You are a strong, independent woman. We love and support you. Just tell him and we will be here for you either way."

Narrator: Katelyn smiled and they all leaned in for a much needed group hug.

Cris: "Can I ask, why is he here if we are on the lamb?"

Katelyn: "He's part of the security detail team. So he's here for you."

Cris: "But you said he was with you for like ten years?"

Katelyn: "You didn't think I was the only child that left their family for the greater good, did you? There are lots of us. This is bigger than you realize. Some of us here. The rest are integrated for later use."

Cris: "Here? Where?"

Katelyn: "We're surrounded. We're safe. Promise."

Cris: "Okay, look. I want to have this conversation now. Everything that is going on has made things super weird. Yes, I could possibly be the next president but that doesn't mean I need to be treated differently. I don't want to lose my family again. I need us united and together. Okay?"

Narrator: "Can do," they said simultaneously. Then they all laughed.

Chapter Ten

Narrator: Dinner went off without a hitch. The family was finally happy again. Geo and Katelyn made eyes across the table all night. Obvious they both had feeling for each other. After dinner was over everyone thanked Geo for his spectacular dinner feast and went to clean their dishes. Geo was putting leftovers in the fridge when Katelyn bounced in wearing her workout clothes.

Katelyn: "You ready?" she asked him.

Geo: "Most definitely," he said with a mischievous grin.

Narrator: Geo talked about a new move he wanted to show her all the way down to the gym. The floors were padded, mirror walls, and loads of exercise equipment. They grabbed some sparring pads and helmets. Geo stretched while Katelyn wrapped her hands and wrists.

Geo: "Are you ready for this? We haven't sparred in a couple of weeks and I want you to know I've gotten better."

Katelyn: "That's hilarious. So you're saying you finally learned to block you face? Haha." She giggled.

Geo: "Whatever, Lynnie," he teased.

Katelyn: "Oh, you're gonna pay for that," she said as they both put their fists up to block their face and walked sideways in a circular motion.

Narrator: Geo ran up and threw a punch. Katelyn saw it coming and reached out to grab his wrists and pull him off balance. She then threw her other arm around his neck to put him in a chokehold. He scrambled for balance and choked and when she gripped him harder, he kicked his leg backwards aiming for her knee. Knowing that move would never land, she jumped back and threw him forward. Back to square one. They danced around each other throwing punches, some landing and some falling through till finally she pulled him down and landed on top of him. She wrapped her ankles around his legs and they struggled with trying to grip each other's arms. She went for his wrists, grabbing one in each hand and holding them to the ground. The fight was over, she had pinned him. They both looked battered and red from the struggle. Thinking they were done, she went to let him go and he slipped his leg out from under her and flipped her off to pin her like she did him.

Katelyn: "Hey, oof. You got m—" Her words cut off as he leaned down and kissed her. He let go of her arms and legs and bent down further to slip his arms around her. Their lips parted and her cheeks became a rosy color.

Katelyn: "Um, wow. That was... (she clears her throat) unexpected." He let her go and got up. Reaching a hand down, he helped her up as well.

Geo: "Yeah, well, I've wanted to do that for a long time. I hope that was okay."

<u>Katelyn:</u> "Yes!" she blurted. "Um, yeah, it's cool. So are you like into me or was that just a onetime thing?" She tried to play it off cool.

<u>Geo:</u> "Oh, it was just a onetime thing, of course." Katelyn looked down thinking she had been played. "Hey, I'm kidding. I like you a lot, Kate. Will you make me a happy man and go out with me?"

Chapter Eleven

<u>Narrator:</u> Flashback to when they were just two kids in a group of fourteen. Some pulled away from their homes and some adopted. They were born to help protect the world one day. Little kids bonding by their need to learn hand-to-hand combat and firearms training. Paired up with a buddy, they would practice for hours. She pinned him down and he could never best her. Seeing as it was her sister who would one day be the president, it was her and her responsibility ALONE to make sure her sister came to no harm lest the world be thrown into a fiery pit of hell by those who chose greed over their promise to protect it. So she fought. She fought hard, swift, and intelligently. She was the best of the 14. She was the only person who could convince her sister to run for office in the first place. It was seen in the vision. If Katelyn didn't convince her sister, then all hope was lost. Life would never be the same. The way things were going in the United States, we wouldn't be a democracy for very much longer but a dictatorship ruled by a man behind the curtain. P.S.: That man was China.

Chapter Twelve

<u>Katelyn:</u> (Oh my God. Did he just ask me out?! Did he just kiss me? I wanna KISS HIS FACE! Wait, stay calm. My cheeks are probably red as a stop sign. Oh. My. God. I can't believe this. Is this really happening? Jeez, focus, FOCUS. He's waiting for an answer. "Yes, I'd love to go out with you...."

<u>Geo:</u> "Great!" he said as he pulled her in for a tight embrace. "You know, I've liked you for a while now, I just didn't know how to ask you. What better way than when I finally beat you at sparring," he said with a chuckle.

<u>Narrator:</u> After putting away the equipment they walked to their rooms to shower.

<u>Katelyn:</u> "Hey, do you want to patrol the grounds with me to make sure were still in the clear?"

<u>Geo:</u> "Yeah, I'll meet you here after I shower," he said as they reached her bedroom.

<u>Katelyn:</u> "Sounds good," she said with a smile.

<u>Cris:</u> "Oh my God. HE did it."

<u>Narrator:</u> Cris had seen it all. She heard every little detail.

Cris: "I'm glad I didn't just walk into the gym like I was going to. I would've ruined the whole thing. I'm so happy for them!! We should throw them a party!!"

Narrator: As Geo and Katelyn showered the rest of the family got together and set up anything they could find for the celebration. Geo knocked on Katelyn's door and waited for her to answer.

Katelyn: "Splash a little of my favorite perfume and ready to go. (knock, knock) That must be him." She opened the door and looked up to find Geo with a big smile plastered on his face.

Geo: "Hey! You ready?"

Katelyn: "Yeah, I just want to stop by the kitchen for a water real quick." They headed down the hallway into the living room. "Huh, why are the lights off?"

"SURPRISE!!!" the family said as Cristina flicked on the lights. She reached to hit play on the stereo and music started coming out of the speakers with a bounce of sound.

Katelyn: "Oh my God, you guys!! What's this for?"

Janet: "We heard you two were together and we couldn't be happier!!!"

They all danced and enjoyed themselves. It all felt like a family after all....

CHAPTER THIRTEEN

The Note

Janet: "What do you mean you forgot to take your multivitamins?! David, we have talked about this too many times."

David: "I know, baby, I'm sorry. I got so excited about the party and our daughter in a new relationship. Especially since I thought this day would never come. That I just forgot."

Janet: "Yes, all those things are great but what about your health? You're sick now and that could get us all sick. Just get back in bed. I'll go see if there's tea in the kitchen."

Narrator: A few hours later David's phone ringing woke him up, caller ID read "Officer Stanton."

David: "Hello?"

Officer Stanton: "Hello, is this David Moore?"

David: Coughed. "Yes."

Officer Stanton: "Sir, your wife was found dead in Loudon County of Tennessee this afternoon. We need you to come in for questioning. I stopped by your home and it looked like no one had been there in quite some time. Where are you?"

David: "What?! Oh my God. Baby, please, no!" he called out. "Baby, are you here?!" he yelled with tears starting to form in his eyes. "I have to go," he said and hung up the phone. He got up out of bed with the sound of wet coughing. He ran downstairs screaming, "CRIS!! KATIE!! GEO!!"

Katelyn came running in from the den with her gun. Thinking there was an intruder. Scoping the living room out, she said, "What, Dad?!"

David: "I just got a call...," he said, crying.

Geo came running in with a look of deep sadness and said, "Kate, I think you need to read this," and handed a piece of paper over to her.

She read aloud: "'Hey, baby, I went to the store to get your favorite tea since we don't have any here. I'll be back soon. I love you. -J.' It's from Mom. She left the bunker...."

Cristina walked in as David said, "She's dead." He braced himself for a cough. "I just got a call from Officer Stanton. My darling Janet is gone. I can't...I can't believe this."

Cris: "What?! Mom's dead?! No! She can't be. I just saw her a few hours ago...Mom...," she said as she dropped to the floor in despair. "Mom, Mom. Please, no."

There wasn't a dry eye in the room. Everyone cried.

Chapter Fourteen

January 20th, 2025, 7:00 A.M.

Dear Diary:

After almost two years of campaigning I'm finally in. Or at least I will be this afternoon. There's a ceremony where I will be sworn in. We're out in the open and everyone knows me now and that I will be the next president. We've come up with a bunch of new laws and rules that will help the world. A lot has changed in the last couple of years. It's actually really scary how things progressed under Joe Biden. So many people lost their lives and so many freedoms were taken away from the American people. But all that will change today. As soon as I am sworn in the new laws and rules will head to the Capitol and will be reviewed and the decisions will be made on whether they go through or not. I don't think we have much to worry about, though, since we fired everyone who was in Congress and brought in a new age of voters. Men and women starting at the age of 18 up to age 59. That way every age group is represented. Since then change has happened for the better. We just have to keep it going in the right direction. I've gotten a lot of questions lately as to why I ran unopposed. I think the reason is clear. No one wanted to be blamed for not being able to clean up this mess that was made. No one wanted the responsibility of taking care of the nation after it had fallen. Because we did. We fell. We fell hard. There wasn't enough people who stood up and stood together. The government manipulated everyone. They drew lines in the concrete to separate the white and colored, rich and the poor, older generations against the newer. It became a battlefield. People were and still are terrified. Majority of them lost their jobs and couldn't provide for their families. Unemployment was at 4.2%, which is 6.9 million people unemployed. Which is not okay. We're going to change it all and I'm not taking no for an answer. I consulted Donald Trump and he has agreed to be my adviser on all presidential matters.

P.S.: It's been a little over two years and we still miss you, Mom. This is all for you and I'm so sorry you didn't get to see where we are today. I love you....

- Cristina River Moore

Chapter Fifteen

Rules, Regulations, and Laws: 2025

<u>Congress Fire Hire:</u> 535 members of Congress were fired and 535 new members were hired. Qualifications include: ages 18 to 59 years old, Knowledge: can pass a 50-question test of previous year's history, Social Media: Social Media Scan (S.M.S.), Citizenship: a citizen of the U.S. for at least seven years and live in the same state they represent.

- No open borders—build a wall.
- Taxes 2% on all products and services everywhere in United States
- Min. wage $20/hr. everywhere even for employees that work for tips (waiters, bartenders) with no taxes taken out
- Grants for small businesses that can't afford this so they don't go out of business
- Every dealership needs to have a product line of cars that are $10,000 or less that will always be approved for. One car per person and the car has to be 100% reliable; otherwise, the dealership pays a fee of the car retail.
- Make more exports and less imports
- Get us out of debt

- Schools: Teach kids how to budget, secure a job, newborn care, DARE, safe sex education, maintaining a household, therapy, how and why to start a business, affirmations/self-esteem, less math.
- Jobs should be picked freshman year and workload should reflect what that job needs from an employee. They are allowed to change jobs but no undecided.
- Vaccine mandates and anything to do with them are to STOP IMMEDIATELY.
- All jobs and monies lost from said mandates are to be given back retroactively from the month of fire date.
- Lower gas prices to min $1.79/gallon and $1.99/gallon max, diesel would be $2.15/gallon.
- All life-threatening procedures and surgeries including labor and delivery will be free.
- Maximum paid leave for every job is 25 days/year.
- Pharmacists are allowed to prescribe medication.
- Doctors are not allowed to prescribe medication, only to diagnose issues.
- Factories that make harmful chemicals and materials have to have a cleanup factory, which results in more jobs.